Aiśvarya Kādambinī

Śrī-Baladeva-Vidyābhūṣaṇā

Translated by
HH Bhānu Swāmi

Title : Aiśvarya Kādambinī

Readers interested in the subject matter of this book are invited to correspond with:

His Holiness Bhanu Swami Maharaj
ISKCON CHENNAI
SRI SRI RADHA KRISHNA TEMPLE
Bhaktivedanta Swami Road,
Off ECR, Akkarai,
Sholinganallur,
Injambakkam,
Chennai-600119,
TamilNadu,
India.

Email : bhanuswamibooks@gmail.com
Web : www.bhanuswami.org
www.iskconchennai.org

Mobile : +91 9790997986
Whatsapp : +91 9790997986

First Edition : 2018 : 100 Copies
Reprint : 2018 : 500 Copies

Printed By Rathna Offset Printers, Chennai - 600 014

This book is dedicated to

HIS DIVINE GRACE
A.C. BHAKTIVEDĀNTA SWAMI
ŚṚĪLA PRABHUPĀDA
Founder-Ācārya :
International Society for Krishna Consciousness

who inspired the world
to take up the path of bhakti.

CONTENTS

Chapter One

Description of the Lord's tripad vibhūti

kābhidhāyai kanakāmbarāyai
śyāmābja-tanvai sarasīruhāyai |
nitya-śriyai nitya-guṇa-vrajāyai
namo'stu tasyai para-devatāyai ||1||

I offer respects to the supreme Lord named Kṛṣṇā, dressed in golden cloth, with bodily complexion of a blue lotus, who is the embodiment of a lotus, decorated with eternal qualities and eternally engaged with Rādhā.

sanātanaṁ rūpam ihopadarśayann ānanda-
sindhuṁ paritaḥ pravardhayan |
antas-tamaḥ-stoma-haraḥ sarājatāṁ
caitanya-rūpo vidhur adbhutodayaḥ ||2||

May Kṛṣṇa in the form of Caitanya, the moon arising in the most wonderful away, who increases the ocean of bliss everywhere, who revealed Sanātana and Rūpa to the world, who destroys all internal darkness, remain victorious!

bahu-bhūma-saudha-sadṛśo vijṣāna-
ghano bahiḥ-stoma-stomāt |
parama-vyomābhikhyo vibhāti viṣṇor
mahādbhuto lokaḥ ||3||

The most astonishing planet of Viṣṇu called the supreme sky, like a combination of many palaces, filled with pure consciousness, exists outside the many layers of the universe.

āste kṛṣṇo yatra nārāyaṇātmā
vyūhair juṣṭo vāsudevādi saṁjṣaiḥ |
kurvan krīḍāṁ pārṣada-grāma-
siddhāṁdīvyad-bhūti-nārasiṁhādi-rūpī ||4||

There resides Kṛṣṇa, in the form of Nārāyaṇa, served by Vāsudeva, Saṅkarṣaṇa, Aniruddha and Pradyumna. Manifesting like Narasiṁha full of spiritual powers, he plays with his many associates.

nityaṁ lakṣmīr yam upāstesva-
nāthaṁnānā-rūpābahu-rūpaṁpareśam |
cit-saukhyātmā sva-samābhiḥsakhībhiḥ
sarveśānā bahu-sambhāra-pūrṇā ||5||

Lakṣmī, having many forms, composed of knowledge and bliss, the ruler of all beings, full of all wealth, constantly worships her master, the supreme Lord having many forms.

dīvyati tad-upari lokaḥ
kuśa-sthalī madhupurī vrajābhikhyaḥ |
yasmin vilasati kṛṣṇo janaiḥ
svakīyaiḥ sa devakī-sūnuḥ ||6||

The planet above this is composed of Dvārakā, Mathurā, and Vraja. There Kṛṣṇa, the son of Devakī, plays with his associates.

dvāravatyāṁ madhu-puryāāca kṛṣṇaṁ
śaineyādyair uddhavādyaiś ca pūjyam |
nānā-sampan-nibhrtāyāṁ pareśaṁ
rukmiṇy-ādyāḥ sambhajante śriyas tam ||7||

In Dvārakā and Mathurā, endowed with various types of wealth, Rukmiṇī and other consorts serve the supreme Lord Kṛṣṇa who is worshipped by Satyāki, Uddhava and others.

śrī-gokule harir asau vraja-nātha-sūnuḥ
śrī-carcite bahu-sakho'sti sa-bhṛtya-vargaḥ|
śrī-rādhikā-priya-sakhībhir adhīśvarīyaṁ
saṁsevate sva-sadṛśībhir ananya-vṛttiḥ ||8||

In Gokula, a place desired by Lakṣmī, the son of Nanda resides with many friends and servants. There Rādhā, the supreme ruler, completely devoted to Kṛṣṇa, is served with by priya-sakhīs similar in nature to her.

evaṁ rūpo harir udbhāti nityaṁ
yad gopālopaniṣat taṁ tathāha |
prādurbhāvaṁsa kadācit prapaṣce'py
aṣcet svāmī sakalāṁśair viśiṣṭaḥ ||9||

This form eternally manifests there. Gopāla-tāpanī Upaniṣad describes him in this way. Sometimes he appears in the material world, accompanied by all his expansions.

madhuraiśvarya-caritra-rūpavattvān
madhurād veṇu-ravāc ca nanda-sūnuḥ |
priyatamatā-pūrṇa-tamāj jana-vrajāc ca
sphuṭam uktaḥ kavibhir vibhur varīyān ||10||

The poets clearly describe the son of Nanda as the best and the most powerful because he has a form and pastimes of sweetness and power, because he plays the flute sweetly and because he is surrounded by devotees possessing the highest love.

Chapter Two

The Lord's appearance in the material world

saṅkarṣaṇo harir atha pralayāvasāne
jīvān udīkṣya karuṇaḥ kṣubhitān samantān |
praikṣiṣṭa sva-prakṛtim aṇḍa-ghaṭās tatas tu
prādur babhūvur uru-bhoga-cayān dadhānaḥ ||1||

At the end of pralaya, the lord as Saṇkarṣaṇa, seeing all the agitated jīvas, glanced at his prakṛti. Then all the universes, possessing great varieties of enjoyment, appeared.

teṣāṁ sva-garbheṣu haris tadābhūt
pradyumnasaṁjṣojanako viriṣceḥ |
bhavanti yasmādbahavo'vatārā
mīnādayo'nanta-guṇā vibhumnaḥ ||2||

The Lord called Pradyumna then appeared in each universe. He gives birth to Brahmā and from that powerful Lord arose many avatāras having unlimited qualities such as Matsya.

antaryāmī vyaṣṭi-jīva-vrajānāṁ
jātas teṣu kṣīradhi-stho'niruddhaḥ |
sārdhaḥ devaiḥ krīḍati prājya-tejās
teṣāṁ śatrūn nāśayan yaḥ samantāt ||3||

Aniruddha, situated in the Milk Ocean, appeared in each

universe. He is the antaryāmī of all the individual jīvas in the universes. Endowed with great powers, he plays with the devatās and thoroughly kills the enemies of the devatās.

yadā yadā rākṣasa-sainya-jālair
dharma-kṣatiḥsyāt praśamāya tasyāḥ |
tadā tadā śrī-mahilaḥ sarāmaḥ
sa vāsudevaś ca bhavet kadācit ||4||

Whenever dharma is injured by the host of demons, in order to alleviate the suffering, Vāsudeva appears along with his consort and Balarāma.

prahlādaṁ yaḥ khidyamānaṁ sva-mṛtyuṁ
vīkṣya stambhād āvīrāsīn nṛsiṁhaḥ |
ugro'dārīt tad-ripuṁ sānukampaḥ
śrī-govindo nanda-sūnuḥ sajīyāt ||5||

Seeing Prahlāda suffering and about to die, ferocious Nṛsiṁha appeared from a pillar and tore apart his enemy. May merciful Govinda, the son of Nanda, be victorious!

svayaṁ hariḥ sa kadācit sadhāmā
sa-pārṣado yadi gacchen nṛlokam |
bhuvo bharaḥ sa tadeyāt praṇāśaṁ
bhaved bahuḥ svajanānāṁ pramodaḥ ||6||

If the Lord personally comes with his associates and abode into the human world the burden of the earth is destroyed and the devotees greatly rejoice.

āvirbhavet prathamaṁ dhāmaviṣṇoḥ
pitrādayaḥ kramatas tatra mukhyaḥ |
paścād asau ramayā tatsamābhiḥ
sārdhaṁ prabhuḥ paramarddhiḥ priyābhiḥ ||7||

First his abode and then chief associates like his parents gradually appear on earth. Later the Lord endowed with all earth appears with his consort and other women of equal qualities.

vidyās tatra svayam eva prabhātāś
cāturyāpy akhilāḥ pārṣadeṣu |
sva-svāpekṣyā hari-bhaktiḥ pratītā
vibhrājeran nikhilāḥ sampadaś ca ||8||

In that place, knowledge and all skills spontaneously manifest in all the associates. Devotion to the Lord according to the individual's inclinations also manifests. All types of wealth manifest for them.

Chapter Three

Description of Vasudeva, Nanda and others who arose in the Vṛṣṇi dynasty

vṛṣṇir vaṁśe devamīḍhaḥ sa o'bhūt
bhārye tasya kṣatriyārye prasiddhe
śūrābhikhyaḥ kṣatriyāyāṁ kumāraḥ
parjanyākhyaḥ sambabhūvārya-kāyām ||1||

Devamīḍha of the Vṛṣṇi dynasty had two famous wives, one of kṣatriya lineage and the other of vaiśya lineage. Śūra was born to the kṣatriya wife and Parjanya was born to the vaiśya wife.

śūrād āsīd vasudevo mahatma
patnī yasya praguṇādevak īsā |
parjanyāt tu vraja-bhūpāt sanando
patnī yasyottama-kāntir yaśodā ||2||

The great devotee Vasudeva appeared from Śūra. Vasudeva's wife was Devakī, endowed with great qualities. Nanda appeared from the king of Vraja, Parjanya. Nanda's wife was Yaśodā, of the highest beauty.

yasmin jāte trideveśair akāri prīty-
utphullair varavāditra-ghoṣaḥ |
sthānaṁ viṣṇor vasudevaṁ saśaurir
mānyo dātā dvija-sevī babhūva ||3||

At Vasudeva's birth, the devatās with ecstatic joy loudly glorified him with the best music. The son of Śūra was respected as the place of Viṣṇu and was thus called Vāsudeva. He was generous and served the brāhmaṇas.

vaiyāsakir yāṁ kila sarva-devatāṁ
jagāda vidvān api deva-rūpiṇīm |
sā devakī viśvadharaṁ maheśvaradadhāra
kukṣau kim ucitram uccakaiḥ ||4||

Devakī, whom learned Śukadeva described as the sum of all devatās, or deva-rūpinī, another form of the Lord, held in her womb the supreme Lord, who holds within himself the universe. How amazing this is!

nandaḥ śrī-kānta-bhakto vraja-dharaṇī-patiḥ śāstravid dharma-
niṣṭhaḥ sāmantaiḥ snigdha-cittair api sacivavaraiḥ śāsanasthair
variṣṭhaḥ | prākārī vara-saudho'parimita-dhavalaś citra-vāditra-
nādair juṣṭo yānair athādyair bahu-vidha-vibhavaḥ sarva-
mānyaḥ sa āsīt ||5||

Nanda was a devotee of Viṣṇu. He was the lord of Vraja, learned in scriptures and fixed in dharma. He was served by affectionate, obedient ministers and neighboring leaders. Living in an excellent palace, having an unlimitedly handsome face, welcomed by various musical instruments, using excellent chariots, endowed with many types of wealth, he was respected by all.

viṣṇur viśvaṁ coṣatuḥ kukṣi-koṇe
yasyāḥ stanyenāpa tṛptiṁ sa bhūmā |
lakṣmīḥ pādau sādarātmā vavande
sā kalyāṇī kena varṇyo yaśodā ||6||

Who can describe auspicious Yaśodā in whose womb Viṣṇu and the universe dwelled, and by whose breast Kṛṣṇa was satisfied, and at whose feet Lakṣmī offered obeisance with reverence?

bandhavo vrajapater bahuvidyāḥ
sāgnayo hari-gurudvija-bhaktāḥ |
sampado'ti-vipulāḥ kila yeṣāṁ
dhenavo bahu-hayāś ca virejuḥ ||7||

The friends of Nanda were very learned, devoted the Lord, elders and the brāhmaṇas, and kept the sacred fire in their houses. They were very wealthy, having many cows and horses.

āsīt sakhā vṛṣabhānur mahīpo
nandasya yo guṇavṛndair varīyān |
kanyā yataḥ praguṇā rādhikā sā
vedaḥ śriyām adhipāṁ yām avocat ||8||

Nanda's great friend was the king Vṛṣabhānu, who possessed a host of most excellent qualities. He produced a daughter, Rādhikā, having the best qualities, whom the Vedas praised as the queen of all Lakṣmīs.

prītiṁ yasmin suṣṭhu taurya-trika-
jṣāḥ prāpuḥ sūtā māgadhā vandinaś ca |
sarvābhijṣā-darśita-sva-svavidyā
yasmāt kāmān lebhire te'bhimṛgyān ||9||

The sūtās, māgadhas and vandis, knowing song, dance and instruments, had affection for Nanda and displayed all their arts to him. From Nanda they obtained whatever they requested.

dānāmbhasāṁ yasya nadībhir
uccair nīvṛn nadīmātṛkāṁ dadhāra |
kalpa-drumāḥ kāma-dughāś ca
śaśvat kāmān samastān vavṛṣur manojṣān ||10||

His kingdom was the mother of rivers, flowing with waters of charity. The desire trees and kāma-dhenus continually showered all attractive objects desired.

govardhano yasya saratnaḥ
śailaḥ sunirjharaḥ kandara-mandirāḍhyaḥ |
puṣpaiḥ phalaiḥ sad-yavasaiś ca
ramyo yathārtha-nāmā vitatāna sevām ||11||

Govardhana Mountain, filled with jewels and beautiful waterfalls, caves and pavilions, fulfilling its name ("increaser of the cows") served him by offering flowers, fruits, and fresh grass.

Chapter Four

Description of Nanda's City

bṛhad-vane yasya bṛhat-kapāṭaṁ
puraṁ bṛhat-saudha-varaṁ babhāse |
ajanmano janma harasya yasmin
babhūva janma praguṇasya viṣṇoḥ ||1||

Nanda's city endowed with a huge palace and huge gates exists within Mahāvana. In that place was born Viṣṇu of great qualities, who though unborn, destroys birth and death.

bhānu-bhūpa-bhavanaṁ yad-antike
kānti-kandala-supuṣ kalaṁ babhau |
preyasī vraja-vidhor maheśvarī
sambabhūva kila yatra rādhikā ||2||

Nearby is the palace of Vṛṣabhānu, replete with all types of beauty. The dear queen of Kṛṣṇa, Rādhikā, manifested at that place.

nandīśvarādrer maṇi-citra-sānor
ūpetyakāyāṁ bahu-nirjharasya |
puśpaiḥ phalaiś cātimanoharasya
puraṁ vrajeśasya mahat tadāsīt ||3|

The city of Nanda is on the jeweled plateau of Nandīśvara,

which has many waterfalls and is most attractive with flowers and fruits.

yasmin vicitrair maṇibhiḥ praṇītā
bhānti sma harmyāṭṭaka-niṣkuṭādayaḥ |
samāna-sūtrair vihitā vipaṇyaḥ
kūpāḥ sarasyaś ca tathā-vidhās tāḥ ||4||

The palaces, towers, and groves shine with colorful gems. The shops are in a straight line as are the wells and lakes.

yad aharan mano ratna-gopurair
urubhir aṣṭabhiś cāru-gopuraiḥ |
rurucire bhṛśaṁ yeṣu rakṣiṇaḥ
kanakabhūṣaṇā bhūpa-pakṣiṇaḥ ||5||

The city is attractive with eight huge, beautiful cow sheds with jeweled arches at the gates. In those sheds are guards ornamented with gold, supporting the king.

yan-madhyamaṁ vraja-pateḥ kila sapta-bhūmaṁ
saudha-rāja-vimalaṁ vilasat-patākam |
vaidūrya-vidruma-masāra-maṇi-praṇītastambhāli-
jāla-valabhī-kula-sat-valīkam ||6||

In the center of the city is the pure palace of Nanda, seven stories high, with fluttering flags. The pillars, lattice work, pinnacles, and roof projections are made of vaidūrya, coral, and sapphires.

nirasta-māyāpi vicitra-māyā
vāso ramāyā nikhilārcitasya |
sabhāḥ sabhānanda-nṛpasya
yasmin samājitā śilpi-varair adīpi ||7||

Though the palace is devoid of māyā, it has various types of māyā (mercy). It is the residence of Lakṣmī, who is worshipped by all people. The palace of Nanda, who gives joy to all, shines unsurpassed by the best of craftsmen.

indra-garva-hara-parva-bhūṣitair
yasya rāja-puruṣair adhiṣṭhitāḥ |
toraṇāś ca kanakādi-nirmitāḥ
projjihānamaṇi- toraṇāvabhūḥ ||8||

Its entrance arches, made of gold and other precious metals, guarded by royal servants whose many ornaments destroy the pride of Indra, defeat arches made of gems.

nalikāvali-vartmabhir jalaughaiḥ
kaṭaka-sthāt sarasaḥ samutpatadbhiḥ |
sadaneṣu saniṣkuṭeṣu yasmin
jala-yantrāṇy udagur vicitra-bhāni ||9||

In that city, water dispensers of various shapes extend to all houses and cottages by using pipes, to bring flowing water from lakes in the hills.

vaidūrya -vajrādi-vinirmitāni
sphurat-patākāny aniśotsavāni |
sadmāni padma-mahilasya viṣṇor
babhuḥ prabhūta-dyutimantir yasmin ||10||

At Nandīśvara the sparkling temples of Viṣṇu, wife of Lakṣmī, has fluttering flags made of vaidūrya and diamonds, indicating a continuous festival.

sthiracayo bṛhad-valayocchritaḥ
kapi- śiraś cayair ati-maṣjulaḥ |
giri-sarāmbubhṛt parikhāṣcito
yad amito lasad-varaṇo varaḥ ||11||

A high firm wall whose upper portions are attractive with many mounds of earth surround the city. It is surrounded by a moat containing water from the Malaya Mountains and has numerous shining, attractive bridges.

bandhana-kraśima-kardama-śabdāḥ
keśa-madhyamṛganābhiṣu yasmin |
cāmarādiṣu ca daṇḍa-ninādaḥ
sormitā-rata-sarita-sarit-sarasīṣu ||12||

In that city the word "tying" means tying the hair, "thin" means slender-waisted, "Mud" means musk ointment. "Stick" (for punishment) refers only to the handle of a cāmara.
"Crying out" refers only to the sound of waves in the moving river or lake.

tīkṣṇatā- tīkṣṇatā-kaṭhinate
yuvatīnāṁ varṇita-kila-kaṭākṣakuceṣu |
chidritā-kuṭilate kramatas te
mauktikeṣu ca kaceṣu yatra ||13||

Sharpness refers only to the glances of young women and hardness refers to young women's breasts. "Having holes" refers to pearls and crookedness refers to curls in the hair.

puraṁ bṛhat sānu-girer upānte
hareḥ priyaṁ tādṛśam udbabhāse |
sarasvatī-juṣṭham adhi pravīraṁ
yad adhyatiṣṭhad vṛṣabhānu-bhūpaḥ ||14||

Near to the huge plateau is a similar large city dear to the Lord, served by Sarasvatī and having many heroes. King Vṛṣabhānu lived there.

Fifth Chapter

Description of the birth of the Lord and his associates

prādurbhūto nandam evaṁ sa kṛṣṇaḥ
śrīmān śaurīṁ cāviveśāmbujākṣaḥ |
tābhyāṁ nyastaṁ vaidha-dīkṣānvitābhyāṁ
tat-patnyau samprāpya taṁ dadhratus te ||1||

Manifesting himself in this world, lotus-eyed Kṛṣṇa entered Nanda and Vasudeva. Their two wives received him by their husbands placing him there through authorized dīkṣa.[1] The two wives then nourished him.

sakhyos tayor deva-garbhatva-yogād
vidyun-nibhā kāya-kāntir babhāse |
saṅgha-satāṁ modayantī samantād
vṛndaṁ dviṣāṁ tāpayantī samāsīt ||2||

Because the Lord had appeared in the two friends, their bodies shone like lightning. They gave joy to the devotees everywhere and gave suffering to the demons.

[1] This means they gave mantra to their wives.

prādurbhāvaṁ bhajamāne mukunde
vāditrāṇi Svayam eva praṇeduḥ |
samphullābhūd vanarājīsamantāt
sārdhaṁ cittair dvija-bhakta-vrajānām ||3||

When the Lord appeared, instruments played by themselves. The forests blossomed with flowers everywhere while the devotees and brāhmaṇas hearts became filled with joy.

namasya-māsi pādmabhe'sitāṣṭamī-niśārdhake
vrajeśvarī sadurgakaṁ hariṁ sukhād ajījanat|
asūta devakī ca taṁ tadaiva kevalaṁ mudā
babhūva moda-saṣcayaḥ satāṁ viśuddha-cetasām ||4||

On the eighth tithi of the waning moon, during Bhādra month, Rohinī constellation, at midnight, Yaśoḍā gave birth to the Lord and Durgā. Devakī gave birth to Kṛṣṇa alone in bliss. The pure hearts of the devotees rejoiced.

dṛṣṭvā putraṁ vasudevaḥ pareśaṁ
hṛṣṭaḥ prādād ayutaṅgāḥ hṛdaiva |
kaṁsād bhīto vraja-rājasya gehaṁ
ninye bhrātus tvaritaṁ taṁ pravīram ||5||

Seeing his son as the supreme Lord, joyful Vasudeva gave unlimited cows mentally in charity. In fear of Kaṁsa he immediately brought his heroic son to the house of his brother Nanda.

hitvā tasminn ātma-putraṁ yaśodā
kanyāṁ nītvā so'bhyadāt kaṁsarāje |
aikyaṁ bimbīr arbhayor vātadābhūd
ekānaṁśācintya-śaktir yato'sau ||6||

Leaving his son at Nanda's house he took Yaśodā's daughter and gave her to Kaṁsa. The two forms of Kṛṣṇa became one through the inconceivable power of Ekānaṁśā.

sūtaṁ vadan parijana-vaktrato hariṁ
pariplutaḥ parihita- veśa-bhūṣaṇaḥ |
acīkaran nija-tanayasya jātakaṁ
dvijottamaiḥ śruta-vidhinā vrajādhipaḥ ||7||

Hearing from his associates that his son was the Lord, Nanda dressed himself with fine ornaments and had his son's birth chart made by the best brāhmaṇas according to scriptural rules.

putrotsave sampradadau sanando
harṣārdito bhūpatir atyudāraḥ |
svalaṅkṛtā vatsa-yutāś ca dhenūḥ
śraddhānvito dve niyute dvijebhyaḥ ||8||

The most generous, joyful king, overcome with happiness on the occasion of his son's birth, faithfully gave two million decorated cows with their calves to the brāhmaṇas.

sapta-prāsād brāhmaṇebhyas tilādrīn raukmaiś
cailai ratna-vṛndaiś ca juṣṭān |
jātaḥ sarvais tatra citro vraje'sau
gāvaḥ sarvā maṇḍitāṅgā babhūvuḥ ||9||

He gave seven mountains of sesame along with gold cloth and gems to the brāhmaṇas. Everyone in Vraja was amazed by this. The cows were all decorated.

somāṅgalyaṁ bhūsurās tatra peṭhuḥ
sūtās tadvan māgadhā vandinaś ca |
vāditrāṇi sphotam āśu praṇedur
gītiṁ nṛtyaṁ cāticitraṁ didīpe ||10||

The brāhmaṇas recited praises on this occasion. Sūtas, māgadhas and vandis offered praise. Instruments suddenly burst into music. The songs and dancing were remarkable.

sutam amita-guṇaṁ niśamya gopā
vraja-nṛpater muditāḥ suramya-veśāḥ |
dhṛta-maṇimaya- bhūṣaṇāḥ suyatnāḥ
sadanam atha bali-pāṇayaḥ samīśyuḥ ||11||

Hearing of the unlimited qualities of Nanda's son, the cowherds of Nanda, joyful, dressed attractively and carefully ornamented with jewels, went to his house with offerings.

vraja-pura-vanitā vicitra-veśā
vara-maṇi-kuṇḍala-nūpuroruhārāḥ |
tam upāyayur upāyanāgra-hastā
nṛpa-nilayaṁ harim īkṣituṁ praharṣāt ||12||

The women of Vraja, in colorful dress, wearing the best gems, earrings, ankle bells and necklaces, joyfully approached Nanda's house with gifts in their hands to see the Lord.

ghṛta-dadhi-rajanī-rasāt kiranto
vraja-nilayā jaya-ghoṣabhūṣitās yāḥ |
vidhi-śiva-sanakādayaś ca tasmin
parinanṛtur nṛpa-catvare'timattāḥ ||13||

The houses of Vraja were sprinkled with ghee, yogurt and turmeric, and resounded with shouts of "Jaya"! Brahmā, Śiva, the Kumāras and others in great joy danced in Nanda's yard.

vraja-patir atha bhūṣaṇair anarghyair
vasana-cayair varasaurabhaiś ca bandhūn |
parijana-sahitān api prapūrṇān
mudita-manāṇḥ sakalān api samārcīt ||14||

Nanda, with joyful mind, worshiped all his friends along with all their associates by giving priceless ornaments, heaps of cloth and excellent perfumes.

tanaya-janma-mahe nṛpatir
babhau racita-kośa-kapāṭavimocanaḥ |
pratijagur nija-vāṣchita-pūraṇaṁ
pramada-sampluti-yācaka-saṣcayaḥ ||15||

The king, on the occasion of his son's birth, opened the doors to his treasury. Receiving all they requested, the people offered praise, saying that all their desires had been fulfilled.

parimitam iva yad babhūva saukhyaṁ
vraja-nagare vraja-bhūpa-tat-prajānām |
tad-aparimitatām avāpa sadyo
yad avadhi tat paramo jagāma kṛṣṇaḥ ||16||

The happiness of Nanda and the citizens which seemed limited now became unlimited when the supreme Kṛṣna came there.

śrī-rāma śrī-dāma-mukhyā babhur
ye pūrva-paścād ujjvalādyāś ca ḍimbhāḥ |
jyotiṣmadbhir bhrājamāno vrajas
tai ratna-vyūhai ratna-sānur yathābhūt ||17||

Balarāma and Śrīdhāmā and others appeared previous to Kṛṣṇa and Ujjvala and younger boys appeared after him. Just as Meru shines with heaps of gems, Vraja shone with the shining boys.

nandādīnāṁ tiṣṭhatāṁ goṣṭhabhūmyāṁ
govindādyair ātmajair lakṣmavadbhiḥ |
nānā-sampat-sevitānāṁ sameṣāṁ
gehe gehe saukhya-puṣjo jajṛmbhe |18||

When Nanda and the cowherds lived in Vraja with Kṛṣṇa and their sons, who were signs of good luck, and were served equally by various types of wealth, the happiness increased in every house.

yāṁ nanda-sūnur manute pumarthaḥ
pumarthabhūto'pi paraḥ pareśaḥ |
rādhādi-rūpādi-guṇair agādhā
babhūva sā dhāmani kīrtidāyāḥ ||19||

Rādhā, most profound for the highest beauty and highest qualities, whom Kṛṣna, the supreme Lord, the goal of all beings, regarded as his supreme being, appeared in the house of Kīrtidā.

janmotsavenaiva jagat sutṛptaṁ
yasyāḥ sureśair api saṁstutena |
pādābja-lakṣmāṇi nirīkṣya nāryo
rameva kanyeyam iti pratīyuḥ ||20||

The universe celebrated her birth with a festival and the devatās celebrated with praises. The women, on seeing the signs on her feet, thought that this girl was Lakṣmī herself.

yāṁ varṇayantaḥ kavayo'pi bibhyuś
candrāravindādi ninindur uccaiḥ |
dhānyena yasyā natibhiś ca śaśvat
pramodam uccair hṛdayeṣu bhejuḥ ||21||

Poets, in describing her, became frightened, and loudly criticized the moon and the lotus. By meditating on her and offering respects to her, they experienced the greatest joy in their hearts.

kaṭākṣa-pātād abhajanta yasyā
vibhūtayaḥ sarva-vidyāḥ prakāśam |
guṇa-vrajān vaktum adhīśvaro'pi
śaśāka no nanda-sutaḥ samastān ||22||

From her glance, all knowledge and all powers manifested. Even Kṛṣna, the supreme Lord, could not describe her wealth of qualities.

sakhyas tu tasyāḥ sama-rūpa-śīla-
guṇāḥ sva-sevātipaṭutva- bhājaḥ |
prādur babhūvur vraja-rāja-hānyāṁ
tadaiva gopa-pravarālayeṣu ||23||

Her friends, who had the same beauty, conduct and qualities, and were skilful in serving her, appeared at that time in the city of Nanda, in the houses of the best cowherds.

Chapter Six

Description of the Pastimes in sequence

ambhoja-cakra-dara-jambu-yavārdha-
candramīnāṇkuśa-dhvaja-pavi-pramukhān vrajeśau |
aṇkān sutasya karayoḥ padayoś ca vīkṣya so'yaṁ
mahān iti paraṁ mudam āpatus tau ||1||

The two parents, seeing the marks of lotus, wheel, conch, jambu, barley corn, crescent moon, fish, goad, flag and thunderbolt on their son's hands and feet, thought, "He is a great personality" and were overjoyed.

dhṛtvā kūṭaṁ kāla-kūṭaṁ ca papa
yāsau dhātrī pūtanā hantum āgāt |
tasyai tuṣṭo veśa mātrāt sa dimbhaḥ
prādād dhātrī-sthānakaṁ śuddhi-pūrvam ||2||

Sinful Pūtanā, having immense poison on her breasts, came to kill the child, but the child, satisfied because she was dressed like a mother, purified her and gave her the position of a nurse in the spiritual world.

kapaṭāvṛtaṁ śakaṭāsuraṁ harir
aṣjasā tam akhaṇḍam |
marutaṁ ca taṁ balinaṁ vibhur
vana-vāsināṁ sukhadaḥ śiśuḥ ||3||

The Lord easily defeated the cart demon who had deviously disguised himself. The baby who was the Lord killed the strong wind demon and gave happiness to the inhabitants of the forest.

yadā yadā mātur aṇke niviṣṭaḥ
sacāpalaṁ divya-ḍimbho vyatānīt|
tadā tadā mātṛ-vargā nyamāṇkṣur
vrajaukasaś cākhila-saukhya-sindhau ||4||

When the small child, sitting on his mother's lap, displayed fickleness, all the women and people of Vraja drowned in an ocean of complete happiness.

gargācāryād ātma-nāmāni bheje gūḍhaṁ
bhāvaṁ vyaṣjayan pūtanāriḥ |
tene'nvarthaṁ corikā-narma-devo
gopālibhir varṇyamānaṁ mukundaḥ ||5||

From Garga, the enemy of Pūtanā received his names, which revealed his hidden nature. Mukunda, who stole and joked with the elder gopīs, made the meanings described in his names successful.

yadā śiśur dhūli-kelau rato'bhūt
mahā-manā sa tadā kāmukebhyaḥ|
dadau mahān dhūli-muṣṭicchalena
prabhur varān amṛtān tān munibhyaḥ ||6||

When the child was absorbed in playing in the dust, the great Lord generously gave the sages who desired to see him the greatest nectar on the pretext of giving them a fistful of dust.

janakam upāgataḥ sadasi nanda-nṛpaṁ capalo dhṛtavara-
bhūṣaṇo madhura-bhāṣaṇo moda-karaḥ|
alika-lasan-masī-kalita-candra-kalaḥ kutukī
harir akhilān vyadhād aticiraṁ viramat-karaṇān ||7||

The fickle child, wearing charming ornaments and speaking sweet words, came to his father Nanda in the assembly, giving everyone great joy. The inquisitive Lord, with gleaming black tilaka on his forehead, made everyone forget their duties for a long time.

kiṇkiṇī-valaya-nūpura-dhārī
niṣka-kuṇḍala-varāṅgadahārī |
pīta-cīna-vasanaḥ sa-ḍimbhaḥ
śiṣjitair api manāṁsi jahāra ||8||

Wearing bells, belt, anklets, medallion, earrings, excellent bracelets and necklace, and fine yellow cloth, he attracted the minds of everyone by the jingling of his bells.

ratha-śibikāṣcito hari-rabhasād uṭajeṣu yadā
paricaritum munīn sva-niratān jananī-sahitaḥ
dhṛta-dadhi-modakādi- balikaḥ sa-balaś cavibhuḥ
pramudam agus tadā subahu te vibudhāś ca parām ||9||

When the Lord as a child went with his mother and Balarāma by chariot or palanquin to the cottages in order to serve the sages who were his devotees, holding in his beautiful hands yogurt and sweets, the sages and the devatās became overjoyed.

bala-kṛṣṇayoḥ sa jagdhau mudād
amīyām samādaduḥ phelām velām
pratītya devāś citram śakuntāḥ
sureśvarāḥ nityam ||10||

How astonishing! Understanding when Kṛṣṇa and Balarāma would be eating, the devatās, disguised as birds, would always joyfully take their unlimited remnants at that eating place.

muṣṇan gavyam gopikānām sa-mitraḥ
puṣṇan kīśān muktavat yaś ca kṛṣṇaḥ
nopālabdho'py uktayāpi sa dhā
tryā prītim nītā sābhyanandot sutena ||11||

With his friends he stole the gopīs' milk products and fed the monkeys liberally. When they told Yaśodā, she did not scold him. Developing more love for him, she was pleased with her son.

mṛtsāprāṣī jṣāpitaḥ svāgrajena
krodhān mātrā bhartsitaḥ pūtanāriḥ |
bhītaḥ svāsye viśvam etat pradarśya
krodhaṁ tasyāḥ śraṁsayann abhyanandīt ||12||

When Balarāma informed Yaśodā that Kṛṣṇa had eaten dirt, she scolded Kṛṣṇa in anger. Afraid, he showed her the universe in his mouth. Her anger subsided and she became happy.

vilokyāparādhaṁ jananyā nibaddho vibhutvaṁ
svakīyaṁ mudv darśayat tām|
vibhajyārjunau tau ca muktau cakāra
svayaṁ baddha-mūrtir batāsau mukundaḥ ||13||

Seeing his offenses, Yaśodā bound him and he joyfully showed her his powers. He broke the two arjuna trees and liberated them, while he, Mukunda, giver of liberation, remained bound to the mortar.

vṛndāṭavīm adhivasan harir ambujākṣaḥ
saṣcārayan sakhi-kulaiḥ saha tarṇakaughān |
vatsāsuraṁ bakam aghaṁ ca jaghāna sadyaḥ
śuddhaṁ vyadhāt kamalajaṁ ca sa jagdhi-mugdhaḥ ||14||

The lotus-eyed Lord, staying in Vṛndāvana, herded the calves with his friends. He quickly killed Vatsāsura, Baka and Agha. Absorbed in eating his lunch he purified Lord Brahmā.

kāliyaṁ bata vimardya sanāgaḥ
sūrajām racitavān pariśuddhām |
nirvivāra khalu gokula-bhājāṁ
bhāvam adbhutam udāram udīkṣya ||15||

The most excellent Kṛṣṇa subdued Kāilya and purified the Yamunā. Seeing the people of Gokula becoming astonished, he prevented Kāliya from staying there.

dīvyan dvandvī-bhāvato'han pralambaṁ
devārātiṁ dhenuka-dveṣiṇā yaḥ |
muṣjāṭavyāṁ dāva-vahniṁ nipīya
vyaktīcakre sādhu-sauhārdam īśaḥ ||16||

While playing, he had Balarāma, enemy of Dhenuka, kill Pralamba, enemy of the devatās, by playing in pairs. Drinking the forest fire in the forest of sedge grass, the Lord revealed his friendship with the devotees.

gopa-kumārī-vasana-nikāyaṁ
skandhe nidadhau sa khalu vimātham |
vīkṣita-sakala-kalevara-śobhaḥ
sūcita-śuddha-janā-mitra-lobhaḥ ||17||

Gazing upon the beauty of their bodies, revealing his desire for friendship with those pure women, snatching their cloth, he placed all the gopīs' clothing on his shoulder.

stotrayatsu na ca yasya kaṭākṣaḥ
sanateṣv api bhaved vibudheṣu |
saṁstuvan vraja-bhuvas taru-saṅghān
sasvaje'timuditaḥ sa bhujābhyām ||18||

Though he did not even glance at the devatās who praised him with reverence, he blissfully embraced the trees of Vraja with his arms, while praising them.

bhuktvānnāni brāhmaṇ īnāṁ mukundaḥ
prādāt tābhyaḥ svāṅghri-lābhaṁ varaṁ saḥ |
saṁskārādyān helayan nātma-bhakteḥ
śraddhām eva khyāpayām āsa hetum ||19||

After eating the food offered by the brāhmaṇas' wives, he blessed them to attain his lotus feet. Rejecting the purification rites of sacrifice, he showed that the cause of devotion to him was faith alone.

kaiśore vayasi harir dharaṁ sādadhre
garviṣṭaṁ tridaśapatiṁ jigāya śakram |
uddrāvaṁ vraja-vanitā-manāṁsi yasmāt
samprāpur madana-kulān ivāgni-puṣjāt ||20||

In his kaiśora age, the Lord lifted Govardhana and defeated proud Indra, lord of Svarga. Because of him, the minds of the gopīs became increasingly passionate, like a host of flames.

gāndharvī vidhir abhavad vrajāṅganānāṁ
dāmpatyai vraja-vidhunā sakhākhilānām |
gīr-vāṇyaḥ kusuma-kiro jagur vicitraṁ
nṛtyantyo dhvanita-mṛdaṅgikāḥ praharṣāt ||21||

Kṛṣṇa, the moon of Vraja, married all the gopīs of Vraja according to gāndharva rites.[2] Heavenly women, showering flowers ,sang various songs, and, while playing drums, danced in joy

vidhiṁ stāvakaṁ bhāvakaṁ candra-cūḍaṁ
tato nirjarān kiṅkarān indra-mukhyān |
harer nanda-sūnor amayanta gopās
tṛṇebhyo'surān kaṁsa-pakṣāśritāṁs te ||22||

Seeing Brahmā' praises, Śiva's devotion, and the devatās headed by Indra serving Kṛṣṇa, the cowherds understood that the allies of Kaṁsa were as insignificant as grass.

śrī-kāntaṁ praṇataika-bandhum atasī- puṣpa-prabhaṁ cid-
ghanaṁ candrāsyaṁ kamalekṣaṇaṁ malayajāliptaṁ lasad-
bhūṣaṇam | citroṣṇīṣam udāra-gaura-vasanaṁ kṛṣṇaṁ
surendrārcitaṁ vīkṣya svānuga-mud yayuḥ paramikāṁ prītiṁ
vrajasthā bhṛśam ||23||

Seeing Kṛṣṇa, the beloved of Lakṣmī, the friend of all beings, blue as a flax flower, filled with knowledge, with moon-like face and lotus eyes, anointed with sandalwood and glittering with ornaments, with colorful turban and bright yellow cloth,

---

[2] Mutual agreement with no ceremonies

worshipped by Indra, the people of Vraja felt great affection and joy for their companion.

atha vrajapatir udīkṣya sad-guṇair
varaṁ hariṁ vinayinam ātmajaṁ mudā |
śubha-kṣaṇe śubha-vidhinā vrajāvane
rajīgamat kila yuva-rājatām asau ||24||

Seeing his humble but excellent son with good qualities, with auspicious ceremonies Nanda joyfully made him the prince of Vraja at an auspicious moment.

balabhadraṁ ca cakāra bhaumikaṁ
vraja-bhūmair harimantriṇaṁca tam |
sadanaṁ tasya sucāru nirmame
sukha-sindhau nikhilān nimamajjayat ||25||

He made Balarāma Kṛṣṇa's minister and owner of the land of Vraja. He made him a beautiful house and made all the people drown in an ocean of happiness.

ādideśa nija-śilpi-kumāraṁ
buddhi-sāgaram apārabalaṁ saḥ |
saudham adbhutatamaṁ racaya tvaṁ
yena rajyati haris tava mitram ||26||

He ordered a young craftsman, an ocean of intelligence with unlimited strength, "Build the most remarkable palace where your friend the Lord can live in splendor."

puru-kānti-valīka-jāla-ramyaṁ
vara-vedī-gṛha-sandhilāṣchitaṁ saḥ |
valitāśrayam ambu-yantra-rāji
vraja-candrasya cakāra sadma sadyaḥ ||27||

He immediately built Kṛṣṇa's palace, with thresholds, altars, rooms, lattices, gleaming roofs and water clocks.

maṇi-baddha-taṭaiḥ sphuṭat sarojaiḥ
śuśubhe yadvimalāmbubhiḥ sarobhiḥ |
ali-guṣjita-maṣjubhiś caturbhiḥ
sphuṭa-prakaraiḥ suniṣkuṭaiś ca ||28||

The palace had four clear lakes filled with blossoming lotuses and jeweled banks, with pleasant gardens possessing blossoming flowers and humming bees.

sa ca racayāṣcakāra girisānuṣu bhūri-vidhān
maṇinilayāṁs tathaiva sura-śilpi-mano-haraṇān |
sapadi sarvais tutoṣa rasikaḥ khalu tatra mudā
saha manasā dadau sa-maṇi-bhūṣaṅa-cela-saṣcayān ||29||

On the plateaus of the mountain, he built many types of jeweled palaces which attracted the mind of Viśvakarmā. Kṛṣṇa was immediately pleased with all this work and with joyful mind gave him piles of fine cloth and ornaments with gems.

smita-vīkṣaṇa-viddha-cetasā
vara-saundarya-sudhā-su-dhāmanī
svajanaiḥ saha rādhikācyutaiḥ
sphuratas teṣu sadaiva medurau ||30||

Rādhā and Kṛṣṇa, the supreme abodes of the highest, sweetest beauty, soft because their hearts were pierced by smiling glances, always shine in these palaces along with their associates.

vraja-nṛpatir jagāma sa yadā saha dāra-kumāra-pārṣador
atha śibikā-hayaiḥ surucirair vṛṣabhānu-puraṁ nimantritaḥ|
sumaṇidharaḥ sa-turya-ninado vara-cāmara-sevito
dyutim atulāṁ vilokya diviṣan nikaro'pi tadā visismiye ||31||

When Nanda, wearing fine jewels, along with his wife, son and attendants, on being invited, went to Vṛṣabhānu's city using attractive palanquins and horses, accompanied by drums, and served by best cāmaras, the devatās, seeing the procession's incomparable luster,became astonished.

adhigamya bhānu-nṛpatir vrajeśvaraṁ
bhavanaṁ ninaya racitārcana-kramaḥ |
paribhojyataṁ bahu-vidhān rasān prabhuḥ
saha-pārṣadaḥ pramudito babhūva saḥ ||32||

When he arrived, Vṛṣabhānu, worshipping him, brought Nanda to the palace and fed him food of various tastes. Vṛṣabhānu and his followers became overjoyed.

sakhi-vṛndair nikhilā samujjihāna-
madhurāsecanakaṁ vilokya kṛṣṇam |
janatā tatra sukhāmbudhau nyamajjat
puru-bhāvās tu viśeṣatas taruṇyaḥ ||33||

Seeing Kṛṣṇa endowed with increasingly sweet beauty along

with his friends, everyone drowned in an ocean of happiness. The young girls particularly developed feelings of great love.

pibator api susmitāmṛtāni rati-
tṛṣṇākulayor adhisnuyunoḥ |
samudaid asitāmbuja-chadābhā taḍid-
abhra-prabhayoḥ kaṭākṣa-vṛṣṭiḥ ||34||

The couple, like lightning and a dark cloud, became anxious with intense desire for pleasure and drank each other's sweet smiles. A shower of glances, beautiful as blue lotuses, arose.

atho bhānu-bhūpo varair maṇḍanādyaiḥ
samarcya vrajādhāra-varaṁ sānugaṁ saḥ |
anuvrajya taṁ sānugas tad-visṛṣṭaḥ
svakaṁ kṛcchrato maṣju bheje nikuṣjam ||35||

Vṛṣabhānu worshiped Nanda and his followers with the best ornaments and then, with his attendants, following Nanda, bid him farewell with difficulty, and entered his attractive bower.

tadā sāravindā jananyā sa-vṛndā
samārādhi sā rādhikābhū ṣaṇādyaiḥ |
hareḥ prema-pātrī yadā rāja-putrī
vraja-kṣema-dhātrī prayātu sahaicchat ||36||

When Rādhā, object of Kṛṣṇa's love, giver of auspiciousness to Vraja, desired to go to Kṛṣṇa, holding a lotus in her hand, she, with her friends, was decorated by her mother with ornaments.

śivikāś ca rathāś ca rukma-celaiḥ
pihitā jālibhir abhrakācakaiś ca |
tad upāyayur ujjvalair lalāmair
bahu-bhāso nṛpa-catvaraṁ tadānīm ||37||

The palanquins and chariots, shining brightly with flashing ornaments, covered with gold cloth, endowed glass and mica windows, quickly arrived in the courtyard.

balair uddhatānām kiśorī-vṛtānāṁ
lasad-yauvanānāṁ raṇad-bhūṣaṇānām|
tadā gujjarīṇāṁ tatir vāgminīnāṁ
mudāyāna saṁvāhanārthādhyatiṣṭhat ||38||

A joyful group of chattering Gujarati women, proud of their strength, gleaming with youth, decorated with jingling ornaments, arrived to mount the palanquins.

samārūḍhayānā balad-bhūrigānāḥ
śanair vījyamānā varaiś cāmarādyaiḥ|
priyā nanda-sūnoḥ pareśasya-vadhvas
tato niryayuḥ subhruvo rādhikādyāḥ ||39||

While loudly singing many songs and being fanned gently by the best cāmaras, beautiful Rādhā and her friends, dear beloveds of Kṛṣṇa, mounted the palanquins and departed.

babhau kāmbavo bhairikaṁ sauṣirāpi
dhvanir maṇgalo rāja-putryāḥ prayāṇe |
lasat-svarṇa-vetrāsi cāpeṣu hastā
dadhāvuḥ puraḥ pārśvato'pi pravīrāḥ ||40||

Auspicious sounds of conches, kettle drums and horns manifested at the departure of Rādhā. Soldiers holding shining golden maces, arrows and bows ran at the sides and in front.

vavau manda-mandaṁ tadā gandhavāho
dadhārātapatraṁ mahad-vārido'pi |
vitenur varaṁ nṛtya-gītaṁ ca
devyo mṛdaṅgādi-nādaṁ nutiṁ cāticitram ||41||

A fragrant breeze gently blew. A huge cloud served as an umbrella. The heavenly women sang and danced expertly, played drums and offered astonishing praise.

phaṇi-phakkikām iva vīkṣya
tāṁ sa-kuṇḍala-nāmapurīm |
dyu-latām ivākhiladāṁ nutāṁ
pramadā hareḥ pramudaṁ daduḥ ||42||

Seeing Nanda's city surrounded by moats, the Lord's women, like fresh creepers from heaven which bestow all desires, became happy.

avatīryatā maṇi-yānataḥ
paritoṇya sārthika-saṣcayān |
praṇipatya gokula-bhūmipāṁ
jagṛhus tato vara-vīṭikāḥ ||43||

Descending from the jeweled palanquins, they satisfied all the persons accompanying them. They offered respects to Yaśodā and accepted from her the best betel nuts.

atha śiṣjitāmṛta-vandita-priya-
mānasāḥ sva-gṛhān gatāḥ|
kṛta-majjanāḥ kamalekṣaṇāḥ
priya-karma tat pratipedire ||44||

The lotus-eyed women, whose jingling ornaments were praised by their husbands, returned their homes, bathed and performed services for their husbands.

sampālayan naicikīnāṁ kadambaṁ
tam pākimaṁ bhāvam eṇī-dṛśāṁ saḥ |
kampākulaḥ sandadhe dīpta-kīrtir
lampaṭa-hṛt sundaro nanda-sūnuḥ ||45||

While herding the cows, beautiful Kṛṣṇa, with passionate heart and shining fame, trembling with longing, developed intense love for doe-eyed Rādhā.

tātam ambu-patitāpanītaṁ
vandito viracītārcana īśaḥ |
āninãya bhavanaṁ puru-tejā
modayan vraja-bhuvaṁ babhāṣe ||46||

Worshipped and praised by Varuṇa, powerful Kṛṣṇa, bringing back Nanda who had fallen in the water and had been taken by Varuṇa, gave bliss to the people of Vraja.

vṛndāraṇya-candikā-vṛnda-ramyaṁ
paśyan vaṁśī vadāyām āsa kṛṣṇaḥ |
āyātābhis tatra gopāṅganābhir
dīvyantībhir maṇḍito'sau babhūva ||47||

Seeing the beauty of the moon beams in the Vṛndāvana forest, Kṛṣṇa played his flute. He became decorated with the brilliant gopīs who had come there.

mādhavyas tā maṣju-taurya-
trikādyair maṣju-rūpyaiś ca kṛṣṇām |
premnānarcuḥ sārthikā saucakāśe anantān
andākhyāyinī vāk tadaiva ||48||

They worshipped Kṛṣna with their sweet forms, sweet music, singing and dancing. This confirmed the statement that the Lord is infinite bliss.

vīṇā-veṇu-mṛdaṅga-nūpura-lasat-kāṣcyādi-nādair abhūt
tātāthai tatathaiś ca tāla-militair nṛtyaiś ca gītaiś ca yat |
citraiḥ pāṇi-vidhūnanais tanu-maṇi-dyotanaiś ca rāsāṅgane tad
vaktuṁ pramavate kathaṁ sukham aho vāg-devatāpi svayam
||49||

How can Sarasvatī herself attempt to describe with ease what happened in the arena of the rāsa dance, with the sounds of flutes, vīṇās, drums, angle bells, and quivering belts, with the dancing and singing, mixed with the rhythms and calls of "tātāthai tatathai", hand movements and shining ornaments?

kuṇḍalitvam anayat sudarśanaṁ
kuṇḍalitvam apahāyan vibhuḥ |
śaṅkhacūḍam api taṁ svam antakaṁ
prāpayann udaharat syamantakam ||50||

The Lord rescued Sudarśana from a snake's body and restored him to his normal self with earrings. He killed Śaṅkhacūḍa and took his Syamantaka jewel.

vraja-vanitā vananta-nirataṁ harim ambuda-sodaraṁ yadā
viraha-dhutāḥ purāṇa-puruṣaṁ jagur ambujalocanāś ciram |
bhuvana-talaṁ tadedam akhilaṁ sarid-uṣṇa-sukhāmbu-saṇkulā
duradhigamā samādhinilayair api haṁsa-kulaiḥ sabhādade ||51||

When the lotus-eyed girls of Vraja, agitated by separation, praised the eternal Lord who was occupied in the forest and who has brother to the clouds, profuse, unfathomable rivers of hot and cold tears covered the whole earth--and even the detached sages rapt in meditation.

vraja-vipine vicitra-vihago hari-veṇu-ravo yadā babhau vidhi-
śiva-śakra-tumburu-mukhā vibudho'pi dadhur vicitratām |
prakṛti-viparyayaṁ tu sarito girayaś ca yayur mithas tadā
vraja-mahilās tu bhejur akhilāś calatā sarasīṣu majjanam ||52||

When the sound of Kṛṣṇa's flute arose like a colorful bird in the forest of Vraja, Brahmā, Śiva, Indra, Tumburu, and all devatās became astonished. Rivers and mountains exchanged their natures. All the women of Vraja in agitation submerged themselves in the lakes.

jāto'riṣṭaḥ kaṣṭakāsāra-vāsī yasmāt
keśī mṛtyu-veśī babhūva |
vyomaḥ prāpa vyomatām eva sadyaḥ
so'yaṁ kṛṣṇo deva-vṛndair vavande ||53||

Kṛṣṇa was praised by all the devatās because Ariṣṭa (who could not be harmed) was put into a shower of difficulty, Keśī (with a long mane) was made to wear death as his clothing, and Vyoma (air demon) was immediately merged with the air.

harir atha mathurāṁ gataḥ sa kaṁsaṁ
praṇihatavān vṛjinaṁ jahāra pitroḥ |
yadu-nṛpam akṛtāhukiṁ pareśaḥ
sapadi kuśasthalikām adhiṣṭhito'bhūt ||54||

Then the Lord went to Mathurā, killed Kaṁsa and relieved his parents of their difficulties. He immediately made Ugrasena the king of the Yadus and established his home at Dvārakā.

kuru-pati-tanayān nihatya duṣṭān
vyadhita patiṁ nikhilasya dharma-putram |
kṣata-khala-nicayo viveśa goṣṭhaṁ
saphalam idaṁ kṛtavān asau tu mābhyām ||55||

Killing wicked Dhṛtarastra, he made Yudhiṣṭhira the king of all people. After killing many miscreants he entered Vraja and satisfied everyone for two months.

Chapter Seven

Description of the Lord's Later Pastimes

śīghra-gaiḥ prati nivedite harau
dundubhiḥ kila jagarja susvanam |
maṅgala-dhvanir abhūd gṛhe gṛhe
kānanāni dadhire madhu-srutim ||1||

When it was announced by quick messengers that the Lord was returning, drums thundered loudly, auspicious sounds arose in all houses and the forests flowed with honey.

udite vidhau pramude dadhe |
vraja-bhūr asau jaladhir yathā ||2||

Just as the ocean rejoices when the moon rises, the land of Vraja rejoiced when Kṛṣna entered.

samupāgate bata mādhave |
aṭavīva sāgamad etatām ||3||

Just as the forest rejoices when spring comes, Vraja rejoiced when Kṛṣṇa arrived.

pariṣasvajire hariṁ pariṣasvajire hariṁ
mudā nija-bhāva-nikhilā vrajaukasāḥ |
sravad-asra-parīta-vakṣaso
vara-nīpa-stavaka-prabhojjvalāḥ ||4||

All the people of Vraja embraced the Lord according to their particular mood of love, while tears flowed over their chests and they shone with the effulgence of excellent kadambas (with hairs standing on end).

tatrāgatās te munayo vanasthā
draṣṭuṁ hariṁ saṁyamino vanasthāḥ |
sampūjitās tena dhṛtātma-bhāvās
taṁ tuṣṭhuvuḥ saṁsphurad ātma-bhāvāḥ ||5||

Sages who lived in the forest and householders with controlled minds came to see the Lord. He worshipped these persons who meditated on him. They praised him with full realization.

sarveśvaras tvaṁ para-muktidas
tvaṁ svātma-pradas tvaṁ svajanānurāgī |
tvam eva vijṣāna-sukhātma-mūrtiḥ
śrī-vatsa-lakṣmī-nilayas tvam eva ||6||

"You are the lord of all beings. You are the giver of the highest liberation. You give yourself. You are attracted to your devotees. You are knowledge and bliss personified. You are the abode of Śrīvatsa and Lakṣmī.

vibhrājitaḥ kaustubha-kānti-vṛndair
jagaj-jani-sthemalayaika-hetuḥ |
acintya-śaktiḥ puruṣādi-rūpo vidhyādayo
deva tavaiva bhṛtyāḥ ||7||

"You are illuminated by many rays from the Kaustubha gem. You are the cause of creation, maintenance and destruction of the universe. You are endowed with inconceivable energy. You are the puruṣāvataras. Brahmā and the devatās are your servants.

govinda nandātmaja-kaṁsa-vaṁśa-
nisū danaḥ śrīdharaḥnaḥ puṇīhi |
śrī-gokulādhīśa jaya tvam uccair
iha svakaiḥ sārdham udāra-kīrtiḥ ||8||

"O Govinda, son of Nanda, destroyer of Kaṁsa's dynasty! O abode of Lakṣmī! Please protect us. O lord of Gokula! May you who have great fame be victorious with your associates!

tava bhaktir acyuta karoti parāṁ
mudira-dyute mudam udāra-maṇe |
pratidehi tāṁ nava-vidhāṁ tad imāṁ
vṛṇumo vayaṁ varam atona na param ||9||

"O Acyuta with the complexion of a cloud! O jewel of generosity! Bhakti to you produces the highest bliss. Please bestow the nine types of bhakti. We do not ask for any other benediction. There is nothing superior to this."

śivikā-ratha-vāji-rājitair
vipineṣu svajanair athāvṛtaḥ |
viharan rasabhojanair atho
mumude'sau parayā śriyārcitaḥ ||10||

Surrounded by his associates, he played in the forests using many palanquins, chariots and horses. Worshipped by the supreme Lakṣmī, he was overjoyed by tasting rasa.

sakhibhiḥ saha dhenu-saṣcayān
sva-samānair guṇa-rūpasampadā |
girirāja-vaneṣu pālayan
vividhāḥ keli-kalās tatāna saḥ ||11||

With his friends who were similar in form, qualities and wealth, he herded the multitude of cows in the groves of Govardhana. He performed various pastimes there.

vanitāḥ sa nitānta-sundarīr niśi
vṛndā-vipine viśan darīḥ|
sukha-sīma-vilāsa-lālasaḥ prabhur
ānanda-mayo'py arīramat ||12||

Eager for pastimes that gave the highest bliss, the Lord, though full of bliss, entered caves in the Vṛndāvana forest at night and enjoyed the exquisitely beautiful women.

etā viṣṇor nanda-putrasya nityā līlā-
nityānanda-mūrteḥ pradiṣṭāḥ |
śraddhāvadbhiḥ kīrtyamānāḥ samantāt
saṁsārāgnipraudham unmūlayati ||13||

These pastimes of Kṛṣna or Viṣṇu, who is the form of eternal bliss, which were taught and glorified by the faithful devotees, completely uproot the fire of saṁsāra.

vidyā-bhūṣaṇa-praṇītaṁ hari-caritaṁ
cit-sukhātmakaṁ hy etat |
parigītaṁ śuka-muninā sadasi
sevyaṁ svarūpam iva ||14||

The pastimes of the Lord presented by Vidyābhūṣaṇa, which are pure knowledge and bliss, first sung by Śukadeva in Parīkṣit's assembly, should be served like the Lord himself.

aiśvaryāparikīrtanād vraja-vidhoḥ kṛṣṇasya ye sādhavas
tāpāgni-pratilīḍha-hṛt-sarasijā mlāyanti śuṣyat-tviṣaḥ |
teṣāṁ tāpa-vimardanāya viśadā śrī-sārvabhauma-prabhoḥ
kāruṇyād uditeyam āśu bhavatād aiśvarya-kādambinī ||15||

Thus, may the spotless Aiśvarya- kādambinī (Cloud bank of the Lord's powers) quickly arise by the mercy of Sārvabhauma Prabhu[3] to destroy the suffering of the devotees whose lotus hearts, consumed by fiery pain, have wilted and lost their complexion because of lack of glorification of Kṛṣṇa's supreme power.

aiśvarye pūrveyam pūrva-parvā
kādambinī nanda-sutāvalambā |
syād bhū-viyat-sindhu-śaśāṅka-
śāke satāṁpriyā tac-caraṇāśritānām ||16||

---

[3] A friend of Baladeva Vidyābhūṣaṇa.

Aiśvarya-kādambinī, concerning unprecedented topics of Kṛṣṇa, appeared in 1701 śakābda. May it be dear to the devotees who have taken shelter of the Lord's lotus feet.

ABOUT BHANU SWAMI

His Holiness Bhanu Swami Maharaja was born in Canada on the 26th December 1948 to the most fortunate Japanese parents. HH Bhanu Swami Maharaja is one of the senior disciples of His Divine Grace A.C Bhaktivedanta Swami Srila Prabhupada, founder acharya of ISKCON, the International Society for Krishna Consciousness. He holds a BA Degree in Oriental fine arts history from the University of British Colombia. He joined the Hare Krishna movement in India in 1970. Initiated in 1971 by Srila Prabhupada, he took sannyasa vows in 1984. Bhanu Swami was personally instructed in the art of Deity worship by Srila Prabhupada, and within ISKCON he has become an authority on the topic. He is a great inspiration for many devotees around the world and he preaches Krishna consciousness in India ,Japan, Malaysia, Australia and Russia.

By 1972, His Holiness Bhanu Swami maharaja already earned credit from Srila Prabhupada for his exact Sanskrit pronunciation, expertise in cooking and excellence in deity worship. He also began to translate Srila Prabhupada's books into Japanese.

A scholar in Sanskrit and Bengali, Bhanu Swami has translated more than twenty significant works of the Gaudiya Vaishnava canon. Many of these works are commentaries from primary members of the Gaudiya sampradaya .

Bhanu Swami is a quiet achiever and has studied a variety of disciplines including martial arts, Reiki healing, Carnatic music (specifically veena). He is a reputed astrologer.

Bhanu Swami's depth of scholarship has enabled him to create presentations on topics like karma, reincarnation, yoga and Srimad Bhagavatam. He continues with this translation service to this day, giving us the nectar from the Bengali and Sanskrit works of the previous Vaishnava acharyas to enhance our understanding of the Gaudiya Vaishnava philosophy. He is also a member of the Governing Body Commission(GBC) of ISKCON.

BOOKS TRANSLATED BY H.H BHANU SWAMI

Ānanda Vṛndavana Campū	- Kavikarṇapūra
Bhakti Rasāmṛta Sindhu	- Rūpa Goswāmī
Bhakti Tattva Viveka	- Bhaktivinoda Ṭhākura
Bhāvārtha Saṅgraha	- Kavikarṇapūra
Brahma Sūtras	- Baladeva Vidyābhūṣaṇā
Caitanya Siksamrta	- Bhaktivinoda Ṭhākura
Daśa Mūla Tattva	- Bhaktivinoda Ṭhākura
Dāna keli kaumudī	- Viśvanātha Cakravartī Ṭhākura
Defining Parakīya & Defeating Svakīya	- Viśvanātha Cakravartī Ṭhākura
Gāyathrī Vyākhyā	- Jīva Goswāmī
Gītā Bhūṣaṇa	- Baladeva Vidyābhūṣaṇā
Gīta-Govinda	- Jayadeva Goswāmī
Gopāla Campū	- Jīva Goswāmī
Gopāla-tāpanī-upaniṣad	- Jīva Goswāmī
Hari Bhakti Vilāsa	- Sanātana Goswāmī
Harināma Cintāmaṇi	- Bhaktivinoda Ṭhākura
Krama Sandarbha	- Jīva Goswāmī
Kṛṣṇa Karṇāmṛta	- Bilvamaṅgala Ṭhākura
Krsnahika Kaumudī	- Kavikarṇapūra
Laghu Bhāgavatāmṛta	- Rūpa Goswāmī
Mādhurya Kādambinī	- Viśvanātha Cakravartī Ṭhākura
Navadvīpa Dhāma Māhātmya	- Bhaktivinoda Ṭhākura
Rāga Vartma Candrikā	- Viśvanātha Cakravartī Ṭhākura
Śrī Aiśvarya Kādambinī	- Baladeva Vidyābhūsanā
Śrī Chamatkāra Candrikā	- Viśvanātha Cakravartī Ṭhākura
Śrī Govinda Līlāmṛta	- Śrī Krishna Dasa Kaviraja Goswāmī
Śrī Īśopaniṣad (Commentaries)	- Madhvācārya, Vedānta deśika, Baladeva Vidyābhūsanā, & Bhaktivinoda Ṭhākura
Śrī Kṛṣṇa Bhajanāmṛta	- Śrīla Narahari Sarakāra Ṭhākura
Śrī Lalitā-Mādhavaḥ	- Rūpa Goswāmī
Śrī Muktā Caritram	- Raghunātha Dāsa Goswāmī
Śrī Vidagdha-Mādhavaḥ	- Rūpa Goswāmī
Ṣaṭ-Sandarbhas (6 Books)	- Jīva Goswāmī
Sat kriyā sāra dīpikā	- Gopāla Bhaṭṭa Goswāmī
Sarartha Darśini(Śrīmad Bhāgavatam) (Canto 1 to 12) in 9 Volumes	- Viśvanātha Cakravartī Ṭhākura
Sārārtha Varṣinī Ṭīkā	- Viśvanātha Cakravartī Ṭhākura
Sri Mādhava Mahotsava	- Jīva Goswāmī
Ujjvala Nīlamaṇi	- Rūpa Goswāmī
Ujjvala Nīlamaṇi kiraṇa	- Viśvanātha Cakravartī Ṭhākura
Vraja rīti Cintāmaṇi	- Viśvanātha Cakravartī Ṭhākura
Vaiṣṇava toṣaṇī	- Jīva Goswāmī